This book belongs to

_____

Ninja Life Hacks®
by Mary Nhin

E C T

Respectful Ninja

Hi, I'm Respectful Ninja. I know my name has the word respect in it, but the truth of the matter is that I haven't always known what respect meant.

This also meant I didn't know how to give it either.

When I was younger, I interrupted people and acted selfishly.

It wasn't it until my friend, Focused Ninja, showed me what respect really looked like that I understood the meaning.

I'm here to share with you what I learned and how you can add respect into your life, too!

To fully understand and show respect to myself and others,
I use an acronym called R.E.S.P.E.C.T.:

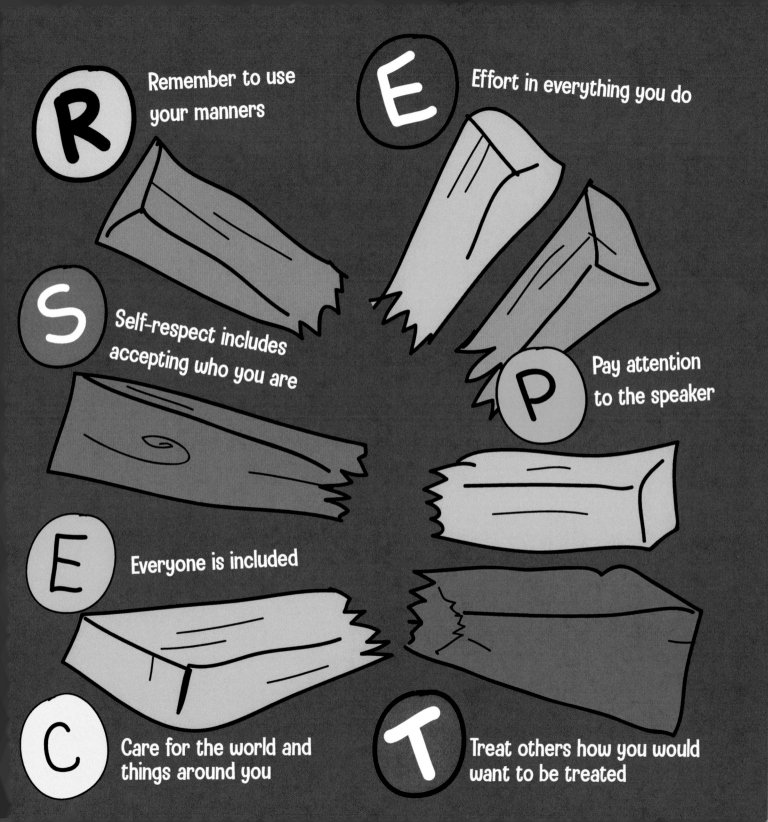

R Remember to use your manners

E Effort in everything you do

S Self-respect includes accepting who you are

P Pay attention to the speaker

E Everyone is included

C Care for the world and things around you

T Treat others how you would want to be treated

R is for remember to use your manners.

E is for effort. Always give your 100% in everything that you do.
It shows respect for your time and other people's time, too.

S is for self-respect. Respect starts with you. Respecting yourself means accepting who you are and who you are not. There is only one you and that is what makes you special.

P is for paying attention to the person who is speaking. We can pay attention by using our eyes and ears to listen and not speaking over someone else.

E is for everyone is included. Inclusivity is a great
way for everyone to have their voices be heard.

C is for care for the world and things around you.

T is for treating everyone how you would like to be treated. This is the Golden Rule!

Check out the Respectful Ninja lesson plans that contain fun activities to support the social, emotional lesson in this story at ninjalifehacks.tv!

I love to hear from my readers.
Write to me at info@ninjalifehacks.tv or send me mail at:

Mary Nhin
6608 N Western Avenue #1166
Oklahoma City, OK 73116

 @marynhin @officialninjalifehacks
#NinjaLifeHacks

 Ninja Life Hacks

 Mary Nhin   Ninja Life Hacks

 @officialninjalifehacks